A STUDY ON ADOPTION OF HEPTACOIN
WORKING PAPER

Written and Conceptualized by

M L Amarnath

GUST- 2021

Chennai • Bangalore

CLEVER FOX PUBLISHING
Chennai, India

Published by CLEVER FOX PUBLISHING 2023
Copyright © M L Amarnath 2023

All Rights Reserved.
ISBN: 978-93-56487-96-3

This book has been published with all reasonable efforts taken to make the material error-free after the consent of the author. No part of this book shall be used, reproduced in any manner whatsoever without written permission from the author, except in the case of brief quotations embodied in critical articles and reviews.

The Author of this book is solely responsible and liable for its content including but not limited to the views, representations, descriptions, statements, information, opinions and references ["Content"]. The Content of this book shall not constitute or be construed or deemed to reflect the opinion or expression of the Publisher or Editor. Neither the Publisher nor Editor endorse or approve the Content of this book or guarantee the reliability, accuracy or completeness of the Content published herein and do not make any representations or warranties of any kind, express or implied, including but not limited to the implied warranties of merchantability, fitness for a particular purpose. The Publisher and Editor shall not be liable whatsoever for any errors, omissions, whether such errors or omissions result from negligence, accident, or any other cause or claims for loss or damages of any kind, including without limitation, indirect or consequential loss or damage arising out of use, inability to use, or about the reliability, accuracy or sufficiency of the information contained in this book.

A STUDY ON ADOPTION OF HEPTACOIN

The following paper is a brief synopsis offering insights into the development and viability of Heptacoin as an alternative for currency-based investment. The paper delves into multi-faceted advantages of investing in Heptacoin, its functioning, and its impact on economy. The intention here is to understand the micro and macro level effects that Heptacoin may have in the arena of investments.

CONTENTS

A Study on Adoption of Heptacoin .... *iii*

1. Growth Of An Idea – Background to Heptacoin 1
2. Germination of the Idea 3
3. Evolution of the Monetary System 4
4. Panini and Encryption – Past Meets The Future 6
5. The Current State of The financial System 9
6. The Mechanism of Notional Value 11
7. The Pricing Mechanism Using Block Chain 13
8. How Does Blockhain Function? 15
9. The Popularity of Cryptocurrecny 18
10. Functionality of Heptacoin and Impact on the Economy 22
11. Future of Regulation - World Cryptocurrency Regulation Protocol (WCRP) 24
12. Focusing on Relevant Indian Payment Mechanisms 26
13. Indian Financial System 29
14. The Indian Cryptocurrency Market 34

CHAPTER ONE

GROWTH OF AN IDEA – BACKGROUND TO HEPTACOIN

The idea revolving around investment in bullion, especially gold, developed within Mr. M.L. Amarnath at a very young age and has its roots in the fascination towards the precious metal. In India, the *Vysyas* are generally believed to be the most progressive class in the world of business. A fifth-generation jeweler and a Vysya himself, Mr. Amarnath has been ingrained with the knowledge of dealing in jewelry (particularly gold), gathered by generations. The knowledge, expertise and fascination embedded in his DNA, has encouraged him to have his own humble ways to deal with gold, whether through collection or investments.

Gold was always relevant in Indian economy. Indian society, with all its elements, has an insatiable appetite for gold which has only grown stronger over the years. Gold, in all its glory, is the very ethos of an Indian family. Gold jewelry finds its due relevance in Dharma Shastra (ancient book of law) in the form of *Stree Dhan,* or the property of a woman as a mark of her personal financial security. Even the age old Ayurvedic treatments consider gold to possess immense value and medicinal properties for treatment of various elements. Whether it is in religious connotations, family heirloom, the tradition of gifting, or merely as a symbol of stature, infatuation for gold is marked in the heart and soul of every Indian (Rani, 2014).

The significance of gold jewelry is undoubtedly illustrious for the Indian society. Although its value of purchase is extremely high, gold jewelry serves as an unproductive asset. Encashing gold jewelry or pledging it for credit results in the loss of the value of the money received in lieu. While banks do lend up to 75% of the gold's worth on pledging, the holder of the jewelry may incur a loss of 40-50% with respect to the money received if it is pledged across the unorganized monetary sector. This phenomenon is often seen across India, owing to the quick liquidity offered by the informal sector (moneylenders, family jewelers, etc.).

Even as a resale commodity, gold jewelry loses its weight value by 4-5% and further loses its monetary worth by 6-7% (Mathew, 2015).

In the age of digitization, financial literacy and the spread of financial accessibility to every nook and corner of the country, the idea of Heptacoin, a cryptocurrency that derives its value from gold, will facilitate a paradigm shift in the investment behavior. Heptacoin retains the sentimental significance of investing in gold yet provides the investor an opportunity to improve financial security and enhance returns on their investment. It not only caters to the provision of investment opportunity to the high and mighty, and the affluent population of the country, but also puts a major emphasis on a pan-India investor market.

CHAPTER TWO

GERMINATION OF THE IDEA

Mr. Amarnath's journey towards developing the idea of Heptacoin, a cryptocurrency that derives its value from the intrinsic value of gold invested in, began in the year 1971 with his humble collection of gold coins. This collection served the purpose of a reserve since the year 1981. A personal experience, a let-down on the use of nation-based currency, and a hit to the business-oriented, sub-conscious mind brought about the notion of a world currency – Heptacoin.

In the year 2001, Mr. Amarnath's forayed into the field of designing and developing doodles and cartoons that simplify the explanation of concepts based out of efficient management such as team building for businesses. During this period, he travelled to of many countries, especially Europe and cutting across borders led to a lot of currency exchange. By the end of these trips an accumulation of loose notes and coins and the whole process of exchange irked him enough to understand that the world needed a common currency which was accepted universally.

CHAPTER THREE

EVOLUTION OF THE MONETARY SYSTEM

*I*n his acclaimed piece of work *Sapiens*, Yuval Noah Harari makes an important identification of the development, rather evolution of mankind. Anthropologically, humans evolved in three stages — the cognitive revolution, the agricultural revolution and the scientific revolution. With the cognitive revolution began the essence of settlements and nascent civilizations. The concept of clans and chieftains, the differentiation of needs, wants and desires, the realization of what one has and what one requires are some aspects of the cognitive revolution that brought about the establishment of the world's first exchange

Mechanism – the barter system, a system established on the principle of reciprocity. Lack of equal reciprocity and low frequency of coincidence of wants lead to the decline of this mechanism (Harari, 2014).

Limitations of the barter system, agricultural revolution, and rise of central economic problems such as what to produce, how to produce, and for whom to produce brought about a new course of exchange in the economic society — the exchange of a standard commodity as a unitary measure of worth for anything and everything that was to be acquired/purchased. This gave birth to the concept of "money", that was centered on the principle of universal convertibility and universal confidence. In India, the most common form of commodity money were the *cowry shells*. Gradual evolution led to the use of precious metals as the first step in the establishment of "Coinage". The first instance of usage of gold coins was in 6th century BC in Rome, Lydia (Harari, 2014).

The system of coinage evolved over centuries, giving birth to legal tenders as a mode financial exchange. Changing factors of economy, emergence of institutions, rise of governments and various other regulatory bodies have changed the framework of today's money. From coins to cash to plastic money, the world is now entering into an environment of digitized finance. Digital wallets, paying-at-go, cashless economy, etc. are some of the most common terms heard in today's monetary parlance.

Amidst the attempts of establishing a new wave of currency emerged the concept of cryptocurrency. A digitally stored currency, that derives its value from an underlying asset and provides the initiator of a transaction the required security and anonymity. The international financial system offers varied types of cryptocurrencies, each differing from the other. For instance, "Petro", a cryptocurrency issued by the government of Venezuela, derives its value from the country's oil and mineral reserves (Spenkelink, 2014).

Heptacoin functions on similar agency. The underlying asset, in this case, is gold. The Indian market of gold investors provides a plethora of avenues to bring the usage of Heptacoin as a powerful and strong digital currency.

CHAPTER FOUR

PANINI AND ENCRYPTION – PAST MEETS THE FUTURE

*A*ncient India has provided the world with distinguished marvels in the form of culture, texts and learned scholars. India has contributed to the world with pure and logical knowledge since the era that fostered the development of writing manuscripts. Today the country is seen from the spectrum of the first world nation, but what cannot be negated is that it has been, since the primordial times, the cradle of classic consciousness.

One such legacy of knowledge was left by a revered Sanskrit philologist called Pāṇini, who was an expert in the field of Sanskrit grammar and linguistics study.

The works of many European scholars, such as Ferdinand de Saussure and Leonard Bloomfield, have been influenced by the manuscripts and descriptive linguistic texts of Pāṇini. The life and origin of Pāṇini's work has been approximated between 6th century BCE and 4th century BCE. His presence was mostly seen in the north- western Indian subcontinent, more specifically in the *Mahajanpada* (greater-state) of Gandhar.

When one hears the name of Pāṇini, the first word that comes to the mind is "Sanskrit", and while his work is based on and around the language Sanskrit, *Ashtadhyayi* is beyond the ambit of language. It has in fact provided extensive insights into various other disciplines. Pāṇini's work on Sanskrit has produced a structure similar to mathematical modeling in algebra. G.G. Joseph, in his *The Crest of the Peacock*, suggested that

Pāṇini's construction of verses provides algebraic reasoning. Like the mathematical functions,

Pāṇini's verses are a way of representing calculated number through words, developing a modern system of numbers, which finds its base in the understanding of language. While the intention was providing a uniform rule book for language, the meticulous calculations of words, their meanings, and its total structure provides basis for modern day coding.

The algebraic construct of Pāṇini's rules was appreciated when a similar generative structure was brought about by Chomsky. Pāṇini took the idea of action as specified by the verb and then developed a comprehensive and calculative theory by providing a thorough context for action, mostly, in terms of its relation to the agents and the situations. This is called *Kāraka* theory and states:

- Which is fixed when departure takes place
- The recipient of the object
- The instrument
- The main cause of the effect
- The basis or location
- What the agent wants to attain (deed, object; and the agent).

The last section of the grammar is one-directional string and set of rules, where a particular rule in the

succeeding sequence ignores all the rules that follow. Pāṇini also uses recursion by letting elements/parts of preceding rules to recur in the later set of rules. These codifications have provided the idea of a computerized program, in philosophy at least, over 2500 years ago.

This schematic coding, leveraged from Pāṇini's understanding of representative sequencing, is the very essence used in encrypting a blockchain mechanism i.e., it is essential for hosting the functionality of cryptocurrencies.

CHAPTER FIVE

THE CURRENT STATE OF THE FINANCIAL SYSTEM

The financial system as we see today is a result of the international agreement that materialized in a historic event in 1945, referred to as "The Bretton Woods Conference". The world was introduced the concept of pegged foreign exchange rates, where currencies were pegged to the worth of gold with governments having the authority to correct any "fundamental disequilibrium". The intention of this act was the creation of a reserve currency that would derive its value from gold and eventually the U.S. dollar became the reserve currency (Farras & Salmeron, 2018).

The advent of cold war, United States declining hegemony, and the liquidity crisis faced by the U.S. led to the event most commonly referred to as the "Nixon Shock" giving us the floating-rate system. The practice of floating-rate system depends on the twin forces of the market to determine the value of a currency i.e., demand and supply. The on-set of a liberal rate establishment mechanism increased the role of the central bank as a regulatory authority to protect the interest of investors (Farras & Salmeron, 2018).

The role of central bank is contradicted with the presence of cryptocurrency. During a cryptocurrency exchange, the transaction is recorded permanently on a digital public ledger using cryptography, a system that helps safeguard information. The process of recording these transactions permanently is called mining, and the digital ledger in which the transactions are recorded is called a blockchain. Blockchain technology uses cryptography to prevent fraudulent transactions such as counterfeiting. Currently, cryptocurrency has no globally recognized, central regulating or issuing authority. The reason central banks consider cryptocurrencies a major hassle is due to the volatility of the digital currency market and anonymity of the source that may be involved in an illicit transaction (Carsten, 2021).

Heptacoin, while a cryptocurrency itself, provides the opportunity to involve the regulatory authorities, without hampering the interests of other stakeholders. Recognition of Heptacoin as a legal tender allows the central bank to regulate money supply in the economy, thereby controlling the inflationary trends. The investable capital in the country can increase by multi-folds due to the sentimental investment made in gold.

The investment in Heptacoin have a similar pattern as seen in the investments of gold-sovereign bonds. The difference being, Heptacoin would not just be an idle investment, it would be moving currency in digital form. The **principle of universality** allows Heptacoin to be recognized internationally as its value is derived from the value of gold, a common measure for pegging a currency, making it acceptable as "World Currency".

CHAPTER SIX

THE MECHANISM OF NOTIONAL VALUE

*I*n an account of his trips to the European countries, Mr. Amarnath relayed that how even though the establishment of European Union has brought about a common currency across the market, a commodity in a franchise of McDonalds can cost 9.9 euros in Belgium, while the same thing would cost 12.5 in Italy. This reflects the differential rate of valuation of a currency and a reason to bring in a common digital currency such as Heptacoin. This would be backed by an underlying investment in **gold as well as Heptacoin Gold coins**. The question now arises about the valuation of gold in this scenario.

The valuation of gold, as explained in detail in further chapters, will be done based on the notional value of the quantum of gold in question, which will be defined by the twin market forces of demand and supply. In such case, the idea of having a high notional value for the gold in concern, as against its intrinsic value would serve as an added advantage for Heptacoin. In a country like India, gold did not need to be promoted, the nature of Indian culture makes it inevitable to invest in gold. While the investment in gold jewelry is obvious and the requirement of cashable liquid investment is also high, right marketing of Heptacoin cryptocurrency and gold coins can help lure investor behaviors in the favor of two avenues. Investment in the gold coin would enable future reserves for jewelry or any other use. An investment in the cryptocurrency would serve as a security-based investment backed by the gold coins.

The "Nudge Theory", a concept of behavioral economics suggests that the decision of a rational group of consumers can be influenced using positive reinforcement. The importance of gold being the positive reinforcement across the globe, a third-party evaluation of Heptacoin gold coin can reflect its notional value much higher than the existing market value of gold. This said, introduction of mining through block chain technology can help converting the value of Heptacoin cryptocurrency at par with the value of the gold coin. Effective marketing would play an important part in this process.

CHAPTER SEVEN

THE PRICING MECHANISM USING BLOCK CHAIN

*T*he valuation of a cryptocurrency is generally affected by three factors namely, utility, scarcity and perceived value. In the case of Heptacoin, these factors would impact the twin market forces with respect to investment avenues in the corresponding Heptacoin gold coins. This highlights the importance of understanding the notional value i.e., the demand and supply patterns in the purchase of Heptacoin. The utility of a Heptacoin is reflected in the financial security backed by gold, the most valuable investment that in its non-ornamental form has high liquidity functionality and provides a steady growth in investment (Mishra, 2021).

The scarcity of gold reflects in its limited availability thereby increasing the aggregate demand in comparison to the aggregate supply. The perceived value of gold, across the globe, is inevitably high due to various reasons established before. This indirectly increases the perceived value of gold-backed Heptacoin. The advent of block chain technology has allowed miners to raise capital in cryptocurrencies and fiat money. This mechanism delves onto the notional value theory of pricing of Heptacoin. The issuance of digital tokens such as Initial Coins Offerings (ICO) or development of smart contracts, provide the investors an opportunity to invest in Heptacoin on the best price offered in the exchange market (Guidici, Milne & Vinogradov, 2020).

The system of notional value helps pegging the value of gold at an exorbitant rate using block chain technology and cryptic mining. This provides an investor the required motivation to invest in Heptacoin. In all similarities, one of the most popular cryptocurrencies of this age, bitcoin, also deploys the method of demand- supply analysis to arrive at the value of every unit of bitcoin, thus pushing the case for notional value-based pricing mechanism.

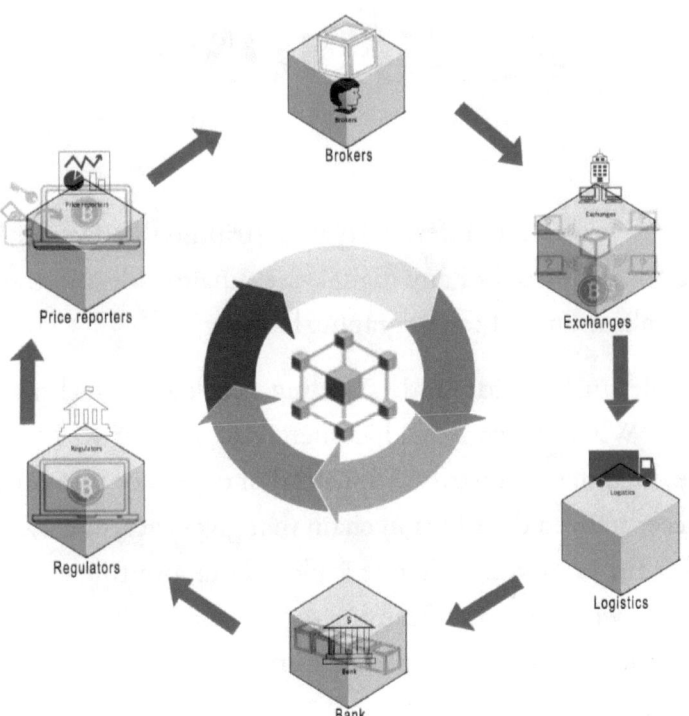

CHAPTER EIGHT

HOW DOES BLOCKHAIN FUNCTION?

*B*lockchain, sometimes referred to as Distributed Ledger Technology (DLT), makes the history of any digital asset unalterable and transparent with decentralization and cryptographic hashing.

A simple analogy for understanding blockchain technology is a Google Doc. When we create a document and share it with a group of people, the document is distributed instead of copied or transferred. This creates a decentralized distribution chain that gives everyone access to the document at the same time. No one is locked out awaiting changes from another party, while all modifications to the doc are being recorded in real- time, making changes completely transparent.

Every chain consists of multiple blocks and each block has three basic elements:

- The data in the block.
- A 32-bit whole number called a nonce. The nonce is randomly generated when a block is created, which then generates a block header hash.
- The hash is a 256-bit number wedded to the nonce. It must start with a huge number of zeroes (i.e., be extremely small).

When the first block of a chain is created, a nonce generates the cryptographic hash. The data in the block is considered signed and forever tied to the nonce and hash unless it is mined.

Miners create new blocks on the chain through a process called mining.

In a blockchain, every block has its own unique nonce and hash, but also references the hash of the previous block in the chain. So, mining a block isn't easy, especially on large chains.

Miners use special software to solve the incredibly complex math problem of finding a nonce that generates an accepted hash. Because the nonce is only 32 bits and the hash is 256, there are roughly four billion possible nonce-hash combinations that must be mined before the right one is found. When that happens, miners are said to have found the "golden nonce" and their block is added to the chain.

Making a change to any block earlier in the chain requires re-mining not just the block with the change, but all the blocks that come after. Therefore, it's extremely difficult to manipulate blockchain technology. Think of it as "safety in math" since finding golden nonces requires an enormous amount of time and computing power.

When a block is successfully mined, the change is accepted by all the nodes on the network and the miner is rewarded financially. One of the most important concepts in blockchain technology is decentralization. No one computer or organization can own the chain. Instead, it is a distributed ledger via the nodes connected to the chain. Nodes can be any kind of electronic device that maintains copies of the blockchain and keeps the network functioning.

Every node has its own copy of the blockchain, and the network must algorithmically approve any newly mined block for the chain to be updated, trusted and verified. Since blockchains are transparent, every action in the ledger can be easily checked and viewed. Each participant is given a unique alphanumeric identification number that shows their transactions.

Combining public information with a system of checks-and-balances helps the blockchain maintain integrity and creates trust among users. Essentially, blockchains can be thought of as the scalability of trust via technology.

CHAPTER NINE

THE POPULARITY OF CRYPTOCURRECNY

𝓑lockchain's most well-known (and maybe most controversial) use is in cryptocurrencies. Cryptocurrencies are digital currencies (or tokens), like Bitcoin, Ethereum or Litecoin, that can be used to buy goods and services.

Just like a digital form of cash, crypto can be used to buy everything from your lunch to your next home. Unlike cash, crypto uses blockchain to act as both a public ledger and an enhanced cryptographic security system. Therefore, online transactions are always recorded and secured.

It can be bought using one of several digital wallets or trading platforms, then digitally transferred upon purchase of an item, with the blockchain recording the transaction and the new owner.

To date, there are roughly 6,700 cryptocurrencies in the world that have a total market cap around $1.6 trillion, with Bitcoin holding a majority of the value. These tokens have become incredibly popular over the last few years, with one Bitcoin equaling $60,000. Here are some of the main reasons why everyone is suddenly taking notice of cryptocurrencies:

The Popularity of Cryptocurrecny

- Blockchain's security makes theft much harder since each cryptocurrency has its own irrefutable identifiable number that is attached to one owner.
- Crypto reduces the need for individualized currencies and central banks. With blockchain, crypto can be sent to anywhere and anyone in the world without the need for currency exchanging or without interference from central banks.
- Cryptocurrencies can make some people rich. Speculators have been driving up the price of crypto, especially Bitcoin, helping some early adopters to become billionaires. Whether this is a positive outcome or not is yet to be seen, as some retractors believe that speculators do not have the long-term benefits of crypto in mind.
- More and more large corporations are coming around to the idea of a blockchain-based digital currency for payments. In February 2021, Tesla famously announced that it would invest $1.5 billion into Bitcoin and accept it as payment for their cars.

Of course, there are many legitimate arguments against blockchain-based digital currencies. First, crypto isn't a very regulated market. Many governments were quick to jump into crypto, but few have a staunch set of codified laws regarding it. Additionally, crypto is incredibly volatile due to those dedicated speculators. In 2016, Bitcoin was priced around $450 per token. It then jumped to about $16,000 a token in 2018, dipped to around $3,100 and has since increased to more than $60,000. Lack of stability has caused some people to get very rich, while a majority have lost thousands.

Whether or not digital currencies are the future remains to be seen. For now, it seems as if blockchain's meteoric rise is starting to take root in reality than pure hype. Though it's still making headway in this entirely new, highly exploratory field, blockchain is also showing promise beyond Bitcoin.

The valuation of Heptacoin, as based on the value of gold, would be done based on the economical paradox of Veblen effect. This will thereby give advantage to the holders of a unit a unique monetary value. The question in sight is how does this logic work with a cold and gold-backed cryptocurrency. As per Michael Foster (2020), shortage is the mother of all development; financial experts frequently refer to this as a case for regular interest. Incredible social orders have collected themselves where naturally happening assets sprout.

Commercial centers were made to permit the exchange of merchandise dependent on their accessibility in the realm.

With the instance of shortsighted labor and products, the standard of financial matters, the legendary laws of interest and supply appeared to hang on most events. Yet, present day culture has developed to show peculiarities.

The laws of interest have seen special cases, most regularly found on account of Veblen merchandise.

A specific class of merchandise whose very nature goes against the law of interest, or "prominent interest" as instituted by nineteenth century market analyst, Thorstein Veblen. It means those products whose request moves the other way of customary merchandise.

Veblen merchandise see their interest go up, as costs increments.

Not your ordinary grain of salt or portion of bread, these merchandises come from the uncommon gathering of restricted and extraordinary resources. Most regularly connected with old fashioned workmanship and uncommon metals, of a 'comprehensive substance,' Veblen products see their worth in the principal law of financial matters — shortage. Furthermore, kid does that drive interest.

One may contend that with time, the case for Veblen products becomes static, or disperses. Alarm products might be substituted or become restricted being used constraining their being a fan to blur.

I'm not inferring that Da Vinci's specialty tracked down a substitute in the banana tapped to the divider, nor am I saying that a 24 carat precious stone on a finger serves no utilization, however it offers a fascinating conversation starter.

The cost of Bitcoin can rise and fall by a huge number of dollars in as little as 60 minutes. For more modest ventures that can occur surprisingly fast. In any case, notwithstanding digital money's famous instability, the allure of computerized cash moves all the more leisurely.

While there is a rich and different corner of crypto whose work is to foresee the value there is an extensively more modest gathering of individuals taking a gander at Bitcoin's cost from a financial point of view. Specifically, opinion around Bitcoin when the cost goes up.

When Bitcoin's value floods, does the interest stick to this same pattern? More critically, when the cost of Bitcoin goes down, does its charm blur with it? In the current week's article, we'll investigate whether Bitcoin has become what financial experts call a Veblen or a Giffen Good.

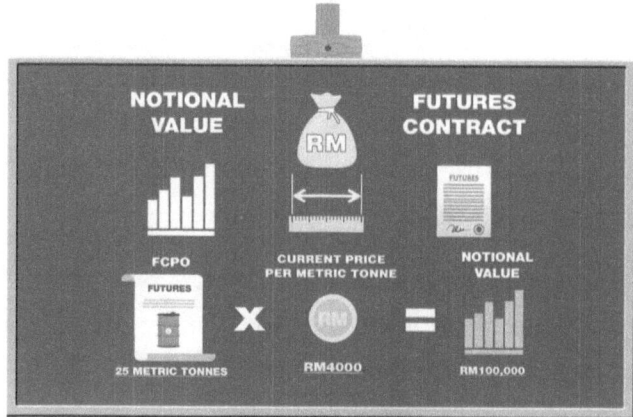

CHAPTER TEN

FUNCTIONALITY OF HEPTACOIN AND IMPACT ON THE ECONOMY

The valuation of gold for the purpose of deriving the value of Heptacoin will be based on Veblen effect, a common economic paradox—the increase in worth or utility of a product is based on the increase in its monetary value. The major question here is, how does this work? The basic concept is that a token or coin is issued that would represent the value of gold (for instance one gram of gold would equal one Heptacoin). The quantity of gold is stored by a custodian, who would preferably be a third party. This can be traded with other coin holders (Carsten, 2021).

At all given times, the price of Heptacoin will always equal the current rate of gold. When Heptacoin reaches a stage of popularity, the price of the coin can potentially increase in value that would be greater than the value of gold. If Heptacoin does not soar in its infancy stage, then the value remains the same as that of gold. This would lead to the development of a "built-in-stop-loss" mechanism. An advantage to hold Heptacoin would be that the baseline of a token will always be equal to the amount of gold (the fixed amount). For this purpose, it is essential to establish transparency between cryptocurrency developers, investors and third- party holders of gold.

The introduction of Heptacoin in the Indian economy would lead to increase in the investment in gold, thereby strengthening the economic gold reserves and contributing the value of INR. This will also improve the prospects of increasing capitalization in the economy. The individual investor would have the opportunity to enjoy usage of a digital currency beyond one's economic territory without the fear of loss of value of it.

CHAPTER ELEVEN

FUTURE OF REGULATION - WORLD CRYPTOCURRENCY REGULATION PROTOCOL (WCRP)

The future of any cryptocurrency is not secure unless it is bound by certain regulatory undertaking. The establishment of standard operating procedures and setting up of regulatory framework ensures that each stakeholder's interest is protected. Along with the establishment of Heptacoin as a world cryptocurrency, it is important to establish a regulatory support system to ensure risk identification and mitigation with respect to transactions of Heptacoin. This would require bifurcation of the entire project into three classifications:

1. Heptacoin Gold Coins
2. Heptacoin Cryptocurrency
3. Heptacoin World Cryptocurrency Regulation Protocol (HWCRP)

Each of the three entities would be operated by three block chain systems, interlinked with one another. The HWCRP will be established with the intention to serve as an advisory body working in proximity with government agencies to ensure that no illicit transactions take place while functioning with Heptacoin.

CHAPTER TWELVE

FOCUSING ON RELEVANT INDIAN PAYMENT MECHANISMS

Unified Payment Interface: Since the wake of the internet era, the greatest number of evolutionary developments have been seen in the banking and finance sector. Constant upgradation of digital economy has led to various innovations to improve the system of payment keeping one thing in mind, the customer's convenience. One such development is the creation of a system called Unified Payment Interface or UPI. This system was first launched in the year 2016 by the National Payment Corporation of India. The Interface lies under the control of the Reserve Bank of India, which is also it's regulating authority.

UPI offers its user the ability transfers funds on an immediate basis using a mobile platform and the internet. Essentially it powers multiple bank accounts into the enfolds of a single mobile application, thereby clubbing various fund routings along with merchant payments under an umbrella platform. The use of this interface requires an application that supports UPI payments, such as Google Pay, Phonepe, BHIM UPI, Paytm, etc. Once the user has the application, a simple verification via mobile number and linking of the user's bank account enables the user to generate a UPI pin. The pin offers security, and the platform offers the customer an easy method of making payments.

But what makes this interface unique? The interface allows for immediate money transfer money transfer on 24 hours a day, 7 days a week and 365 days a year with a single mobile application that can access different user registered bank accounts. A single click and a two-factor authentication system provides for a seamless and secure transaction. It has provided the regulatory authorities the ability to keep track of all digital transactions and avoid any maleficence and fraudulent embezzlement of finances across the country.

The parties generally involved in a UPI based transactions are the payer, the payee, the remitter bank, the recipient bank, the beneficiary bank, NCPI as the apex record holder, and merchants.

The universal application of the interface, its ease of use, availability round the clock and the fact that it is a step towards a paperless, rather cashless economy is what makes it extremely appealing. As per a reporting in *Business Today*, as of October 2020, NCPI's measurable success with UPI in India has led to opening of avenues to establish UPI in various Asian economies such as UAE, Singapore and Malaysia. This would be a beneficial step keeping the expatriates and tourists, on both sides, in mind allowing clean flow of revenue through track-able means. Evidently the success of UPI has seen small folds and is now expanding across countries, reducing the geographical

National Electronic Fund Transfer: The National Electronic Fund Transfer system, also referred to as NEFT, is a nation-wide electronic funds transfer system that was established by the Reserve Bank of India in the year 2005. The agenda behind the establishment of NEFT was to have a centrally controlled and monitored system to facilitate a secure, efficient, reliable, and economical system of fund transfer and monetary in clearing in the Indian banking sector. This revolution was a step toward achieving a paper-less banking environment. This system was developed indigenously by the Institute of Development and Research in Banking Technology, with the assistance provided by the RBI.

Essentially NEFT allows the transfer of funds from one NEFT enabled bank account to another. Currently it is the most popular method of fund transfer in India because of the 24 hours a day-7 days a week-365 days a year transfer avenue offered by this technology. As long as the IFSC for a bank account holder is available, any NEFT enabled account holder can transfer funds without any hassle. The NEFT system also caters to individuals who do not have a NEFT enabled account. Such individual may make a cash deposit at an enabled bank branch with essential details. The only restriction in such a case would be a cap on the amount that can be transferred i.e., INR 50,000.

In an otherwise regularly conducted NEFT transfer, there is minimum or maximum cap on the amount that can be transferred to another NEFT enabled bank account holder. A transfer within the ambit of the same bank's account takes only a couple of minutes, but transfer between different banks may take a longer duration to materialize. A very commonly neglected fact about the NEFT system are the charges applicable on a NEFT transfer. There are no charges to the recipient beneficiary. In addition to this, any NEFT based transaction initiated on an online basis via mobile banking or internet banking is also not chargeable.

NEFT as a service platform is not merely a transfer avenue. It also can be used for the purpose of loan payments, making EMI payments, settling credit card dues, etc. NEFT allows one to perform most banking functions without the requirement of either party's physical presence or the use of any physical monetary instruments as long as the accounts in question are pre-validated. In essence, NEFT is a platform that ensures secure real-time transactions for the parties involved in a simple and efficient manner.

CHAPTER THIRTEEN

INDIAN FINANCIAL SYSTEM

The Indian Financial System is one of the most important aspects of the economic development of our country. This system manages the flow of funds between the people (household savings) of the country and the ones who may invest it wisely (investors/businessmen) for the betterment of both the parties.

The services that are provided to a person by the various financial institutions including banks, insurance companies, pensions, funds, etc. constitute the financial system.

Given below are the features of the Indian Financial system:

- It plays a vital role in the economic development of the country as it encourages both savings and investment
- It helps in mobilizing and allocating one's savings
- It facilitates the expansion of financial institutions and markets
- Plays a key role in capital formation
- It helps form a link between the investor and the person saving
- It is also concerned with the Provision of funds

There are four main components of the Indian Financial System. This includes:

1. Financial Institutions
2. Financial Assets
3. Financial Services
4. Financial Markets

Let's discuss each component of the system in detail.

1. Financial Institutions

Financial institutions act as a mediator between the investor and the borrower. The investor's savings are mobilized either directly or indirectly via the financial markets. The main functions of financial institutions are as follows:

- A short-term liability can be converted into a long-term investment
- It helps in conversion of a risky investment into a risk-free one
- It also acts as a medium of convenience denomination, which means, it can match a small deposit with large loans and a large deposit with small loans

The best example of a financial institution is a bank. People with surplus amounts of money make savings in their accounts, and people in dire need of money take loans. The bank acts as an intermediate between the two.

The financial institutions can further be divided into two types:

- **Banking Institutions or Depository Institutions** – This includes banks and other credit unions which collect money from the public against interest provided on the deposits made and lend that money to the ones in need.
- **Non-Banking Institutions or Non-Depository Institutions** – Insurance, mutual funds and brokerage companies fall under this

category. They cannot ask for monetary deposits but sell financial products to their customers.

Further, financial institutions can be classified into three categories:

- **Regulatory** – Institutes that regulate the financial markets like RBI, IRDA, SEBI, etc.
- **Intermediates** – Commercial banks which provide loans and other financial assistance such as SBI, BOB, PNB, etc.
- **Non-Intermediates** – Institutions that provide financial aid to corporate customers. It includes NABARD, SIDBI, etc.

2. Financial Assets

The products which are traded in the financial markets are called financial assets. Based on the different requirements and needs of the credit seeker, the securities in the market also differ from each other.

Some important financial assets have been discussed briefly below:

- **Call Money** – When a loan is granted for one day and is repaid on the second day, it is called call money. No collateral securities are required for this kind of transaction.
- **Notice Money** – When a loan is granted for more than a day and for less than 14 days, it is called notice money. No collateral securities are required for this kind of transaction.
- **Term Money** – When the maturity period of a deposit is beyond 14 days, it is called term money.
- **Treasury Bills** – Also known as T-Bills, these are government bonds or debt securities with maturity period of less than a year. Buying a T-Bill means lending money to the government.
- **Certificate of Deposits** – It is a dematerialized form (Electronically generated) for funds deposited in the bank for a specific period of time.
- **Commercial Paper** – It is an unsecured short-term debt instrument issued by corporations.

3. Financial Services

Services provided by Asset Management and Liability Management Companies. They help to get the required funds and make sure that they are efficiently invested.

The financial services in India include:

- **Banking Services** – Any small or big service provided by banks like granting a loan, depositing money, issuing debit/credit cards, opening accounts, etc.
- **Insurance Services** – Services like issuing of insurance, selling policies, insurance undertaking and brokerages, etc. are all a part of the insurance services
- **Investment Services** – It mostly includes asset management
- **Foreign Exchange Services** – Exchange of currency, foreign exchange, etc. are a part of the foreign exchange services

The main aim of the financial services is to assist a person with selling, borrowing or purchasing securities, allowing payments and settlements, lending and investing.

4. Financial Markets

The marketplace where buyers and sellers interact with each other and participate in the trading of money, bonds, shares and other assets is called a financial market.

The financial market can be further divided into four types:

- **Capital Market** – Designed to finance the long-term investment, the capital market deals with transactions which are taking place in the market for over a year. The capital market can further be divided into three types:
  - (a) Corporate Securities Market
  - (b) Government Securities Market
  - (c) Long Term Loan Market

- **Money Market** – Mostly dominated by government, banks and other large institutions, this type of market is authorized for small-term investments only. It is a wholesale debt market which works on low-risk and highly liquid instruments. The money market can further be divided into two types:

  (a) Organised Money Market

  (b) Unorganised Money Market

- **Foreign exchange Market** – One of the most developed markets across the world, the foreign exchange market, deals with the requirements related to multi-currency. The transfer of funds in this market takes place based on the foreign currency rate.

- **Credit Market** – A market where short-term and long-term loans are granted to individuals or organizations by various banks and financial and non-financial institutions is called credit market.

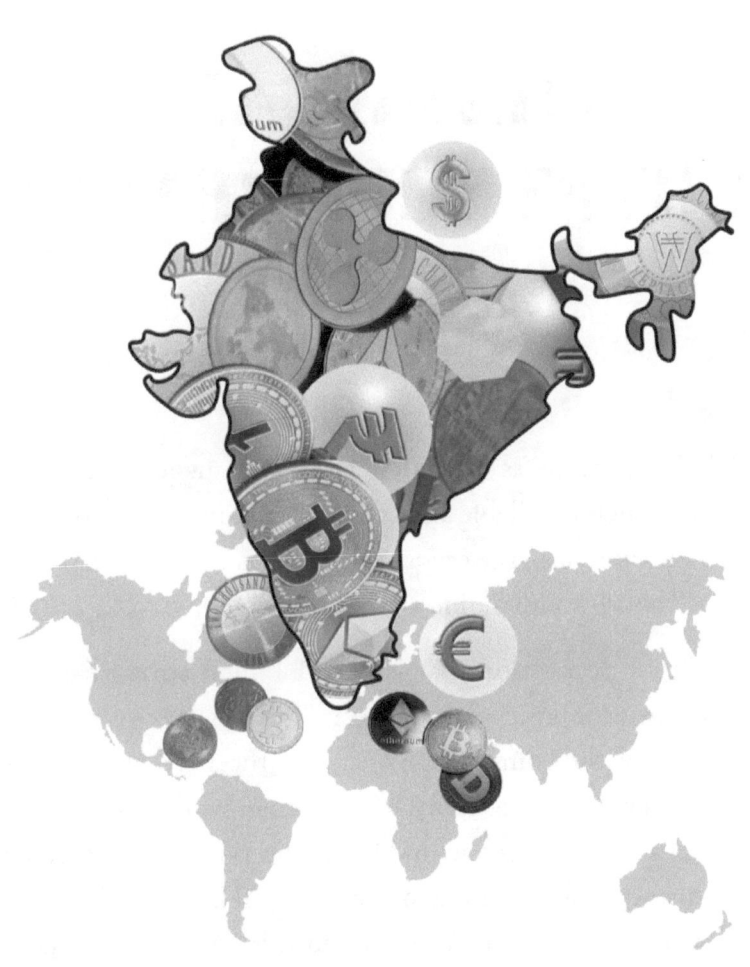

CHAPTER FOURTEEN

THE INDIAN CRYPTOCURRENCY MARKET

The Global Landscape as of March 18, 2018, suggests that there are 1564 cryptocurrencies available and traded in about 9422 exchanges. The market capitalization of all the cryptocurrencies is $275,797,435,861 i.e., $275 billion. The 24-hour volume was $ 18,207,953,654 i.e., $18 billion.

India with a population that is over 1 billion strong has been on something of an economic renaissance in the last few years. Such has been the extent of the country's growth that the IMF has called it the fastest-growing, emerging economy. More than 40 percent of the country's population has access to telecoms and internet services. A country steeped in mystery, history, and culture is not one to fall behind when it comes to technological advancement. Bitcoin and other cryptocurrencies have been operating within the country for several years now. This article looks at the state of the Indian cryptocurrency market. As early as 2012, small scale Bitcoin transactions were already taking place within the country.

These were still early days in the development of Bitcoin when only crypto hobbyists were interested in Bitcoin. By 2013, Bitcoin was beginning to gain a level of popularity that was spreading across many countries. That year, a few businesses began to accept Bitcoin payment. A vintage era pizza shop called Kolonial in the Worli area of Mumbai became the first restaurant service in India to accept Bitcoin payments.

The demonetization policy also led to widespread criticism of the mainstream financial scene in the country. In the space of 24 hours, 86 percent of the country's paper currency in circulation had been rendered valueless by virtue of a single government proclamation. Realizing that fiat money isn't exactly "real" money since it isn't backed up by anything, Indians began to seek alternative currency models. Many Indians, especially those in the 40 percent bracket with access to the Internet began to take up Bitcoin and other cryptocurrency investments. The 2016 demonetization policy may have spurred the adoption of cryptocurrencies among a considerable portion of the population but realities soon began to emerge that have stifled the growth of the market in the country. Despite its vast population, India only contributes 2 percent of the total global cryptocurrency market. Name Price Market Cap Bitcoin $8254.8 $ 142.2 B Ethereum $ 528.33 $ 52.97 B Ripple $ 0.65492 $ 25.92 B Litecoin $ 151.22 $ 8.52 B Monero $ 208.7 $ 78.16 M Neo $ 58.98 $ 260.1 M capitalization.

The small role being played by such a large economy can be attributed to the high cryptocurrency prices and the RBI-led government crackdown. The general level of prices of cryptocurrencies in India is on the high side.

Market rates are relatively higher by as much as 5 to 10 percent compared to the global average. This means that Indians can only get involved in peripheral participation in crypto trading as far as international crypto exchange platforms are concerned. Lack of large-scale mining facilities and government restrictions on international money flow also make it significantly difficult for Indians to transact with many of the large foreign crypto exchange platforms. The Reserve Bank of India

(RBI) has been consistent in warning citizens of the risk associated with cryptocurrencies. While the government of the country hasn't banned cryptocurrencies, they haven't exactly been endorsing it. The coming months will reveal the direction in which the crypto market will move as far as India is concerned.

The impact of cryptocurrencies on the Indian economy is clearly depicted as the prices of cryptocurrency market are now falling. Indian government has made it clear with their stand of not providing a legal status for cryptocurrency in India. The reason for this kind of a decision from government hails from, first, the decentralized transactions in cryptocurrencies are difficult to trace which could be advantageous for the hackers, criminals and also for terrorist activities. The second reason being cryptocurrency market could be a leading competitor for the banking service industry. Cryptocurrency like Bitcoin has become popular in India like other nations as the volume of Indian rupee being traded in cryptocurrency have been at the highest post-demonetization.

Research shows that the volume generated by the rupee dominated cryptocurrency is the third largest volume traded after American Dollar and Yen. The demonetization policy of 2016 may have encouraged the implementation of cryptocurrencies amongst a substantial share of the population, but realities rapidly began to come out that have subdued the growth of the market in the country.

www.ingramcontent.com/pod-product-compliance
Lightning Source LLC
LaVergne TN
LVHW091536070526
838199LV00001B/93